SWEET GRASS TALKING

For Kellie —

My thanks for your
lifelong friendship and your
activism in the world.

Peace Ametané'e Roman Nose

Poems

Renée Ametané'e Roman Nose

First U.S. edition 2017

Editor and Publisher   Laura LeHew

Proofreaders: Karen Locke
                       Nancy Carol Moody
                       Keli Osborn

Cover Art: This piece of art is made from beads and thread on
                       denim. It was created without a pattern, from the
                       artist's heart and mind, reflecting her time at Bear
                       Butte. It is also reflected in poetry in the poem, "My
                       Strength."

                       "My Strength" beadwork on denim;
                       © Renée Roman Nose 2017

Copyright © 2017   Renée Ametané'e Roman Nose

Uttered Chaos
PO Box 50638
Eugene, OR 97405
www.utteredchaos.org

ISBN: 978-0-9889366-7-6

For my grandfather, Eugene Blackbear, Sr., who believed in me and asked me to write "Sand Creek Massacre," telling me, "If we don't remind them of what they did to us, they'll forget."

For my husband, Brian Patterson, who shows endless patience with my love of poetry and art, and whose love inspires me.

For my children, Stephanie Spiering Ironheart, Wokawokamosh Roman Nose, Raven Hunter-Canales, LuLu Canales, Tatiana Crawford and Danae Black.

For my editor, Laura LeHew of Uttered Chaos, thank you for understanding and appreciating my poetry, as well as for your ability to immerse yourself in the stories behind them.

To George Pamp, who encouraged me to publish my work, and who asked me to title my second book, *Sweet Grass Talking*. Thank you for believing in me and thank you for being my friend. In your honor, instead my first book carries your title.

For everyone who ever shared their stories with me, for everyone who ever asked me to write for them, for everyone who ever shared their hearts, their homes, their laughter, their joys, their sorrows, their tears, their food, and their jokes. For all my relations.

Hahoo.

CONTENTS

Every society needs these kinds of sacred places because they help to instill a sense of social cohesion in the people and remind them of the passage of generations that have brought them to the present. A society that cannot remember and honor its past is in peril of losing its soul.
~Vine Deloria, Jr.

MY STRENGTH

I see the stallion
    thundering hooves striking
        powerfully driving him
            muscles bunch and respond
                conquering the steep mountain with ease

He storms past me
    his strength
        flowing into me
            renewing me physically
            spiritually

The stallion gallops determinedly
    thundering up the mountain
        in my mind
            protecting me
                strengthening me

The storms that surround me
    fall before him
        thundering hooves scattering
            the inconsequential
                the fear and doubt

I feel the stallion
    in my heart
        enveloping my soul
            encompassing me
                his hide blinding in its purity

The storms which once ravaged
    my heart and my life
        devastating all in their path
            now swept aside
                by a greater purpose

Our land is everything to us... I will tell you one of the things we remember on our land. We remember that our grandfathers paid for it - with their lives.
~John Wooden Legs, Cheyenne

THE WARRIOR

Strength radiates from within
Obvious even to a casual observer
A sensitivity that he strives to conceal
To all but those closest to him
Makes him all-the-more precious
To those he trusts
Talents many and varied
A heart as strong as his people
Pride as deep as his roots in this land
With an awareness of his own responsibility
To the generations to come
As well as those of today
Cares not for those whose lives
Are wrapped in facades
Roots firmly in reality and awareness
Commits to preserve the irreplaceable
That which was almost destroyed
By greed
Precious and few to nurture,
Protect, prolong, and strengthen
By hope.

A warrior is challenged to assume responsibility, practice humility, and display the power of giving, and then center his or her life around a core of spirituality. I challenge today's youth to live like a warrior.
~Billy Mills

NATIVE SON

You brighten my life with your smile
      your heart as warm as the sun
Each day you struggle
      with harassment at school
For your long hair
      for your Native heritage
I listen to your words of frustration
      and shed my tears inside
While my words, chosen with care,
      encourage you to be strong
I try to balance my anger
      with reason and kindness
While wondering why the kids at your school
      aren't taught the same by their parents…
I see you growing, changing
      last year you were shorter than me
This year you tower over me
      calling me *little!*
You make me laugh with your jokes
      your teasing ways
So sweet and gentle
      all big feet, heart, and awkward bones
Growing every day
      in more than height.

WINTER TALES

Oral history, some call it
Family time, bonding one to another
The story so well remembered that our lips move in unison
    as we silently mouth the words
Like water rushing to the freedom of the ocean
We listen with our hearts, the familiar words falling from our storyteller's
    lips,
Sharing our culture, our history, our pride in who we are
As we share our stories with other generations
All gathered 'round
From small babes to grandparents
All anxiously awaiting the next adventure shared
In this lively way
The firelight dances
As it reflects over our faces and our selves
Granting warmth and comfort
On a cold winter's night
The stories make us laugh
Until we hold our sides
We feel sorrow at the tragedies faced by a hero
The night pulls around us
As we move closer to hear the soft words
Spoken so gently now
Then we laugh at the sudden appearance
Of that trickster Coyote!
The stories end and we all head home
With the stories still dancing in our heads
In the distance the waves crash on the rocky shore
Comforting us in their continuity
Lulling us to sleep as Coyote
Winds his sly way through our dreams…

TOO INDIAN

He said that I was *too Indian*
When he said goodbye
And I watched him walk away
With tears in my eyes
I let him go
I knew that he was right
The bridge between our races
Could not be spanned by me alone
He needed to meet me in the middle
By building from his side
The bridge remains unfinished
Except for the long span from my side
I worked on it
For so long.

Tribal enrollment will continue to be a hot topic in Indian Country as we work toward self-determination and fight for our sovereign rights. Tribes have the right to determine who is, and who is not, eligible for enrollment without outside interference and judgment. Being Tribally enrolled doesn't mean you get a check from the government every month; it doesn't mean you get scholarships; it doesn't mean you get great health benefits. It is an acknowledgment of your people that you belong to them and they belong to you, that you have a responsibility to your people and they to you. It conveys membership, responsibility, and recognition of one of our own.

THE CARD

What Tribe are you from?
        people ask with interest
Can you prove it?
        they ask rudely
Yes, I answer
        I have a card
My Tribe, my people
        many of the Native people
Of this land of the free
        and home of the real braves…
Are required to have
        a Tribal I.D.
Does it say who you are?
        it says what Tribe
Does it give you money?
        no, my job gives me money
Doesn't the government do that?
        no, just me.
Anyone can make a card
        only I can provide for me
What I am
        I am Cheyenne.
My people, my Tribe
        that's who I am.

THE LOST GENERATION

We are the lost generation
Adopted out
Farmed out
Given away
To be raised by others
Not of our culture

We feel an emptiness
A chasm between those we love
And those we come from
Reaching out to find who we are
Where we come from
We are returning to our people

Learning about ourselves
Filling in the gaps
Answering the questions
That have plagued us for so long
Through so many sleepless nights…
We don't ask for anything

But acceptance
We are one of your own
Gone for awhile
The blood will tell
It's the blood
That brings us home.

For too long, this nation forcibly took our children from us; in many cases they were taken as young as 5 years old and weren't allowed to return home until they were 18. Families were discouraged from visiting, and children were deliberately sent to boarding schools that were great distances from their homes. Too many of them were subjected to mental, physical, and sexual abuse by those who were entrusted with their education and care. Too many of them lie in cemeteries at those schools, never to go home again.

HOME FOR CHILDREN

I hear the whimpers, soft cries at night
When they lock us all up, it can't be right
Torn from our mothers' arms, carried to this place
Pale strangers, not one familiar face
Our hair cut so short, falling to the ground
Surrounded by braids, scattered all around

My voice cries out in my Native tongue
I am slapped to the ground, kicked like dry cow dung
English! Speak English! The white man yells to me
What foreign place is this? What country?
Indian Boarding School it says outside on the sign
A "home" for Native children, stand in line
Wait to be whipped, wait to eat
Wait to be given hard shoes that cramp your feet

Missing your moccasins, your family and friends
Praying for an escape, waiting for the end
To go home at last, a stranger in a familiar land
Unable to speak, no longer can you understand

You've lost your language; the red road is no longer clear
Force fed the white path too long, why were we here?
Who made such a law, such a choice?
What God approves of such injustice, who denies us our voice?
· Happy children once, now lost fools
Locked away in homes, Indian Boarding Schools

Turned us neither red nor white
Stole away our carefree youth, our birthright
Searching for a path when both roads are closed to us
Now we have no world, they have stolen our way, our path, our focus
Indian, Apple, White, what will it be?
For the lost generation of you and me.

EXPRESSION

don't you see that you are living
on stolen land?
that the immigration bill
you support wholeheartedly
would have applied to the first boat people
from the Niña, the Pinta, the Santa Maria…
can you not feel the injustice
of a nation that offered citizenship
to its first citizens
in 1924
this same nation despised those Native men
who declined to fight in World War I
for a country that denied them
their language
their fertility
their culture
their children
their land
their religion
only to grant them citizenship in 1924?
a country that had hunted us to virtual extinction
only 40 years before
Indian Wars
Seminole Wars
Sand Creek
Little Big Horn
Battle of the Washita
Trail of Tears
Wounded Knee
the Black Hills
        Native land
buried under miles and miles of concrete.

In a meeting with a professor from Rollins College several years ago, it became apparent that our cultural differences were not going to be bridged by either of us; the cultural divide was too great.

ROLLINS COLLEGE ANTHROPOLOGIST

In a democracy, the majority of the citizens is capable of exercising the most cruel oppressions upon the minority.
~Edmund Burke

You may study us
        your whole life through
Understand us?
You never will
Safe in your literary ivory tower
        protected from reality
While starving Native children
        knock ineffectively at your door
Bones are your forte
        while you let the living lie dying
you study your version
        of our past
Compare the alcoholism problems
        we undoubtedly have
With the student drinking problems
        you see on your privileged campus
The hopelessness and despair
        you parallel to your society
Try to fit our Native bodies
        into your white molded version
Comparing sovereignty
        to termination
Denying the rights
        we have fought so hard for
        Anthropologist awake!
Today is fleeting
The real Natives are before you
Fighting for our rights
For repatriation
        our ancestors
        the future of our children
        for the seventh generation
Continuing the fight
        that you refuse to see.

We are the product of our communities, our families, those who have gone before us, the ancestors who fought and died and those who survived so that their children could live.

DEPTH

Reach deeper
  he said to me
Pull from within
  to see who you are
Let your blood
  and the blood
Of your ancestors
  speak
Speak to you
  speak to us all.

In March, 1957, on a sleepy Sunday afternoon, the falls were destroyed, dynamited, to become the backwaters of The Dalles Dam. This also destroyed a way of life that had endured for thousands of years, a summer meeting place for Tribes from all over the West as they came to trade for part of the estimated 15-20 million salmon that once traveled through the falls every year. The once mighty "June hogs," those salmon weighing over 50 pounds, are no more, thanks to the installation of the Grand Coulee Dam, one of more than 250, which prevented salmon from returning to their spawning grounds.

HISTORY LESSON

United States Territorial Expansion
     the book declares to every student
Teaching them that it was right
     and proper
As well as courageous
     to invade an inhabited land
You teach confusion
     as you teach national pride
How much pride is gained
     by stealing? Lying? Cheating?
Murdering? Raping? Dismembering?
     Treating us as strangers in our own land?
Requiring us to be "federally recognized"
     by your federation of course!
We already know who we are
     what we are
We are the Native people
     of this land
Of these
     Americas
We are the First Americans.

They made some low wide gallows on which the hanged victim's feet almost touched the ground, stringing up their victims in lots of thirteen, in memory of Our Redeemer and His twelve Apostles, then set burning wood at their feet and thus burned them alive.
~Bartoleme De Las Casas

WWJD, indeed.

Bartoleme De Las Casas, *Brief Account of the Devastation of the Indies*. N.p., n.d. Web. 19 June 2017.

INHERITANCE

We are trapped with a blanket
not of our own making.
All Indians. All different Nations.
Identified by one misnomer, cursed
for all time by Columbus.
The lost, stubborn, greedy, murderous
fool who sought India
but found us instead.
From the Oregon Coast to Long Island
From Alaska to Argentina, we are the Native sons
The Native daughters, the inheritors and
caretakers of the land.
Inheriting nearly lost legacy
Stolen bit by bit,
Relative by relative
By the invading hordes from across the sea
Denied our religion in America
for too long.
Denied our land in South, Central, and North America.
Fighting to regain that which was swindled
Lost, promised as long as the grass grows
As long as the river flows.
So much for promises…

According to national statistics, Native people are incarcerated at the second highest rate of all Americans, a number only exceeded by African Americans. Statistically speaking 709 out of 100,000 Native people are incarcerated. 1815 per 100,000 African Americans are incarcerated. Native people comprise only 2.0 percent of the entire population of the United States of America. In Montana, where Native people are 6 percent of the population, the prison population is 16 percent Native. This poem was written for our family members who are incarcerated, many of them because they couldn't afford an attorney, competent or not.

Greenfeld, Lawrence A. and Steven K. Smith. *American Indians and Crime*. N.p.: n.p., 1999. Web.

Initiative, Prison Policy. "Recommended Reading:" *U.S. Incarceration Rates by Race | Prison Policy Initiative*. N.p., Web. 14 May 2017.

Dehaven, James. "Report: Native Americans Make up Disproportionate Share of Rising Montana Prison Population." *Missoulian.com*. N.p., 21 Apr. 2016. Web. 14 May 2017.

PATCHWORK-QUILTED CROPS STREWN
ACROSS THE LAND

My eyes hunger for the beauty of her face
In all its varied wonder
From the striking plains to sun-drenched seas
My eyes hunger for the beauty of her face

Drinking in the glory of the mighty redwoods
Silent sentinels watching over her
Gazing at majestic mountain peaks and lush valleys
My eyes hunger for the beauty of her face

Cobalt blue lakes beckoning in welcome
Pulling me to their stone strewn shores
To walk by rushing rivers, tumbling, twisting, twining
My eyes hunger for the beauty of her face

My eyes hunger for the beauty of her face.

MY ELDERS

I listen to your stories
Avidly
Your knowledge a gift to all of us
That you share
In spite of your age
The strength that you once had
Now visible in your will
Maybe not as much in your physical self
Yet you don't let that slow you down
As you travel
To dances
To memorials
To ceremonials
Visiting friends, family
Sharing your love
Your warmth, kindness
Your wonderful humor
Bringing laughter to those around you
Bringing the joy of your love
To your family and friends.

The old 'Indian' teaching was that it is wrong to tear loose from its place on the earth anything that may be growing there. It may be cut off, but it should not be uprooted. The trees and the grass have spirits. Whatever one of such growth may be destroyed by some good 'Indian', his act is done in sadness and with a prayer for forgiveness because of his necessities...
~Wooden Leg, Cheyenne

WIND SONG

The wind carries messages
      for those with ears to hear
The trees carry signs
      for those with eyes to see
The forest tells stories
      to those who can read
The eagle beckons
      to those whose spirits are free.

DIGNITY

He walks into the arena with care
Each step causes his body pain
Yet…his mind rejoices
Rejects the stresses
Trembling legs threaten to fail
And do not…
His back slightly bowed by time
A face deeply carved by life
By love, loss
Survival
His will stronger than flesh
His heart and soul
In each step
Carries him with grace
Slow, painful
His movements reflect
The beauty and strength
Of the drum
Enduring
Everlasting
Inspiring

SABU

the gentle giant, they called you
       known far and wide for your helping hand
for your humor, your goodness
       they knew you well from coast to coast
Still these many years later
       I meet people who knew you
when you walked the land
       when you were the pow wow clown
To me you were unknown
       and remain that way still
except for the stories of you
       my heart craves and cherishes
From those who knew you
       loved and respected your protective heart
My father, the stranger
       I wish I knew you then…

According to statistics gathered by the Indian Health Service, Native Americans (American Indians and Alaskan Natives) have an overall death rate, of injury-related deaths, twice that of all other racial and ethnic groups in the country. Native women are 3.5 times more likely to be raped than women of any other group. The suicide rate of Native American men over the age of 20 is four times that of Native American women in the same category.

End of Horn, Pamela and Hearod, Karen. "Screening and Assessment for Suicide Prevention." Https://www.ihs.gov/telebehavioral/. N.p., 21 June 2016. Web.

Rosay, André. *Violence against American Indian and Alaska Native Women and Men: 2010 Findings from the National Intimate Partner and Sexual Violence Survey.* Washington, DC: U.S. Department of Justice, Office of Justice Programs, 2016. Web.

MY FRIEND

I picture you still… heart whole and body strong
Your enthusiasm boyish, I remember hiding my smiles
At your unconsciously charming ways

I long for those days as we sit outside in the lobby
Cold, clinical and too clean. Waiting… praying…
Willing you to live

We cannot go back, but we can pray for you
To go forward with us in whatever way the Creator decrees
Prayer is all we have now

Prayer and hope, we cling to both and each other
With all our strength, and we hope,
That it will be enough…

THE FALL

My tears fall unbidden
as another warrior is taken
lost to the despair
lost to those left behind
the pain encompasses us all
the grief holds us
in its icy embrace
no comfort in the closeness
no relief from the suffering
that we reluctantly share
only the question remains

I was given one of my names by a Potawatomi elder. He still holds a place in my heart and a speed dial number on my phone. His friendship and wisdom continue to resonate in my life. Hahoo, George Pamp!

FRIENDS

Thanks to AT&T Potawatomi to Cheyenne,
Reaching out across the miles
Connecting our thoughts, sharing ourselves
One culture similar to another
Shared loss, shared land
What was once ours, is no longer
What is left is what we fight to keep
Reaching out beyond the boundaries
To share our dreams
To hold on and expand our horizons

WELCOME

Crushed by the crowds
Towering concrete trees block the sun
Thick, dark pollution stunts the view
The very air an enemy

The mountains close around me protective
Full of life and hope
Shelter from the storms of a modern world
An escape from the jungle of the city

My lungs and life
Fill grateful for
Cleansing breath
Clean, bright air

Choose your friends by their character and your socks by their color, choosing your socks by their character makes no sense, and choosing your friends by their color is unthinkable.
~Anonymous

IMAGINE

Your mind's eye envisions
Children running free
Laughter fills the air
Wafts toward you
On a hot Oklahoma day
Children of many nations
Cheyenne, Ponca, Osage
Black, Chinese, White
Play, laugh in harmony
Their hearts see not color
But friends.

BROADEN YOURSELF

I'm writing a book of poetry
About Native issues and historical events
Broaden your topic, he says to me
No one wants to read about Natives,
No one is really interested in them!
I fought back the anger that was bursting to be free
I held back the words that blistered my tongue
Measured my thoughts
Weighed them so very carefully
Then I spoke
Slowly and succinctly,
We are interested.

Alcoholism is a disease that strikes indiscriminately, young, old, wealthy or poor, people of all nations; it affects almost everyone's life. Native people work to limit accessibility to alcohol, as in efforts made in Whiteclay, Nebraska, (population 30) where four small businesses sell approximately four million cans of beer each year while the business owners refuse any sense of responsibility for the alcohol related incidents and deaths that happen on the road between Pine Ridge and Whiteclay, once called the deadliest road in America. The vast majority of those sales are made to Tribal members leaving the dry rez of Pine Ridge and journeying over to Whiteclay to buy "white man's poison."

Hammel, Paul. "Critics, Defenders of Whiteclay Beer Sales Testify at Hearing; 4 Stores Reapplying for Liquor Licenses." *Omaha.com*. N.p., 05 Jan. 2017. Web. 14 May 2017.

NIGHT WALKING

Brother, I see you night walking in the sun

The stagger in your step
Stark contrast
With the smile on your face
Lost in the misery, pain, hopelessness
Of your life
Torment flooded by the bottle

Brother, I see you night walking in the sun
The laughter that others barely hide
At your condition
Pulling me to you
To guide
To protect and defend
My back is straighter
My spine firm as my heart
Right or wrong, we are all related

You are my brother
You are my self
My torments are within you
Open wounds bleeding freely
My tears fall within me
At your pain
At the pain within us all
Our torment flooded
By the bottle

Brother, I see you night walking in the sun.

CALLING THEM HOME

When the Creator, in His infinite wisdom
Calls a child home
We grieve
For the loss of one so loved
Given to us for such a brief time
To be cherished and loved
The precious joy
The gift of that love
The child that will remain forever young
In our memories
In our hearts
Our child will never know
The cares of this world
The burdens will never be heavy
Never bow his heart or mind
As he lives on
Safe in the warm embrace of the Creator.

All birds, even those of the same species, are not alike, and it is the same with animals and with human beings. The reason WakanTanka does not make two birds, or animals, or human beings exactly alike is because each is placed here by WakanTanka to be an independent individuality and to rely upon itself.
~Shooter, Teton Sioux

ROUND DANCE

My hand reaches out to you
Inviting you to join me in the circle
The round dance, friendship dance
Your reluctance is apparent, understood
But you reach up to me and take my hand
I help you to stand up and lead you
Into the circle
Guiding your footsteps
As others guided mine
With patience, understanding
And humor
We dance together
For this moment in time
The differences in our cultures
Is forgotten
For this moment we are joined
In friendship
And harmony.

This was written for a friend of mine, many years ago, but it could have been written for *many* of my sisters and friends... aayyy...

THE SINGER

He had flashing dark eyes
        long black hair
His teasing ways won me over
        his gentleness made me stay
A voice that caught me
        held me still
The drumbeats
        matched those within me
His songs
        keep echoing in my heart.

SNOW ANGEL

Long black hair
        Smooth copper skin
                Fall into the snow
                        Fall with me… again

The importance of the oral tradition of our ancestors continues to be very powerful and respected in our communities as a way to teach lessons, to entertain, and to retain our culture.

STORYTELLER

She walks with dignity into the arena
      the director has called her
She has graciously agreed to share
      a few stories of her people
Sharing them with those who take time to hear
      those who are touched by her words
The ones who listen beyond the story
      to the lessons behind it
The reason for the story
      is masked, but there nonetheless
She shares it with all
      but only the listening hear
Smile and laugh, or learn
      they see her time worn face
The countless laugh lines
      the ready smile and open heart
She reaches out to all
      but only a few can hear.

A MOTHER'S LOVE

A mother's love cannot be bought
it is given with each thought
to the children borne and the children given
and fills each day of living.
The warmth and care to each one
the playful moments, stories, all the fun
form a bond that endures through time
between you and yours, I and mine.

THE FAN

It was a little thing
She had other fans now
Many finer and newer
But to the young girl
It was a jewel beyond compare
The Cherokee woman gifted it to her

To my eyes it needed work
To hers it was perfect
She clasped it in her little hand
Carried it with evident pride

When we got home
I gently pried it from her sleeping fingers
As she held it firmly to her warm chest
Carried her in and laid her to sleep
Then sat down to see the fan

It had seen better days
But there was beauty still
In the strong feathers
And the making of it was good
So I took on the task

Working late into the night
Cutting leather
Sewing by hand
Giving back what time
Had taken away

The morning brought an early rise
To my sweet daughter
Running into my room,
Asking, *Where is my fan?!*
Jumping up and down

Instantly awake
I took her little hand in mine
And led her to the fan

That she would now carry
That was truly her own

Her joy was immeasurable
My late night was doubly repaid
By the shining dark eyes smiling at me
And the little brown hands
Caressing the fan.

A Nation is not conquered until the hearts of its women are on the ground. Then it is finished, no matter how brave its warriors or how strong their weapons.
~Cheyenne proverb

NATIVE BLOOM

Rose by name
        rose by heart
You can feel that come through
        from the start
With beauty unchecked
        by time
She is dignity and honor
        clearly defined
Dancing with honor
        moving with style and grace
The pride of her people
        shown on her face
She is a Native rose
        Rose is her name
She is a Native woman
        too strong to tame.

Dedicated to Rose Olney

AUTUMN

After all the wild summer
       Love away
And teach me
       An evening song

THE JOURNEY

the wind will know your name
the wind
the wind will
      know
your name

the wind will
      caress your cheek
blow softly
      ease the journey
warm your face
      for
the challenges
      ahead

RACISM

I am standing in line at Kmart
       Waiting like the good girl I've been brought up to be
Waiting in line at Kmart
       For my turn to be helped by the clerk
Watching one white person after another
       Be helped and sent on their way
While I wait and wait
       And see more white people
Step up before me
       Confused and frustrated
I finally ask to be waited on
       While the white people around me
Look on with frank disapproval
       I am embarrassed at their judgment
At my own forwardness
       Then angry that this is how it is.

I am a red man. If the Great Spirit had desired me to be a white man he would have made me so in the first place. He put in your heart certain wishes and plans, in my heart he put other and different desires. Each man is good in his sight. It is not necessary for Eagles to be Crows. We are poor... but we are free. No white man controls our footsteps. If we must die... we die defending our rights.
~Sitting Bull, Hunkpapa Sioux

ANGER

It makes me so angry!
        my Mohawk friend said
His voice filled with frustration
        after reading a history of America's
Treatment of their
        indigenous people
He threw down the book
        as if to rid himself of the images
Of our ancestors
        fighting and dying
Of disease striking indiscriminately
        of the U. S. Cavalry striking with violence
Planned and calculated
        deliberate
Extermination
        the anger within him
Lives within me as well
        how could our people
Have been so brutalized
        by those who claimed to be civilized?
How can today's descendants
        forget so easily?
Not understanding
        our anger
Our frustration with the continued inequities
        the continued lies and broken promises
Could it really be possible
        not to realize that they too would fight
For their country
        their beliefs
Their religious freedom…
        can we push it all aside
As they do?
        should we all just forget?
Can the descendants of the African slaves
        push aside their heritage?
Can any oppressed people
        forget being hunted to virtual
Extinction?

1995

Save a Fish, Kill an Indian,
the bumper sticker proclaimed from a white pickup…

Welcome to the land of the free
Where the fishing rights and treaties
Last as long as a whisper on the wind
Promises made to our grandparents
For as "long as the grass shall grow,
as long as the rivers flow"
(or until we find something we want
on your land)
Uranium, oil, gold
All for what?
For a land you cannot possess
Only rent for a short time
How can you own
The earth, the sky, the sun?
The air that we breathe
That you are destroying day by day
Technology has brought us so far
That some cannot leave their homes
Now we are all paying for your deeds
It is not too late to recover
From all that has been wrought
Not too late to live at peace
With the earth and your brothers
Brothers and sisters of all nations

Custer Died for Your Sins,
said a bumper sticker on a rez car…

U.S. Constitution - Article 6
Debts, Supremacy, Oaths

All Debts contracted and Engagements entered into, before the Adoption of this Constitution, shall be as valid against the United States under this Constitution, as under the Confederation.

This Constitution, and the Laws of the United States which shall be made in Pursuance thereof; and all Treaties made, or which shall be made, under the Authority of the United States, shall be the supreme Law of the Land; and the Judges in every State shall be bound thereby, any Thing in the Constitution or Laws of any State to the Contrary notwithstanding.

The Senators and Representatives before mentioned, and the Members of the several State Legislatures, and all executive and judicial Officers, both of the United States and of the several States, shall be bound by Oath or Affirmation, to support this Constitution; but no religious Test shall ever be required as a Qualification to any Office or public Trust under the United States.

ASTONISHMENT

My face a reflection of surprise
A dear friend, non-Native
Expresses her opinion to me
You should pay taxes, she says
You are an American, just like everyone else
We do pay taxes, I respond,
Although I don't think we should
I agree, I am an American
I am a First American
Native, Indian, however you prefer
We have paid over-and-over again
In millions of acres lost
In millions of lives lost
We have paid in blood
To those who helped themselves
To our country
To those we welcomed, fed
Helped to survive
Only to be repaid
In treaty after treaty
Each one worth as much as the paper
They were written on
Each paper promise forgotten
By the Great White Father
In Washington
Who did it for our own good…

The white people, who are trying to make us over into their image, they want us to be what they call "assimilated," bringing the Indians into the mainstream and destroying our own way of life and our own cultural patterns. They believe we should be contented like those whose concept of happiness is materialistic and greedy, which is very different from our way. We want freedom from the white man rather than to be integrated. We don't want any part of the establishment, we want to be free to raise our children in our religion, in our ways, to be able to hunt and fish and live in peace. We don't want power, we don't want to be congressmen, or bankers.... we want to be ourselves. We want to have our heritage, because we are the owners of this land and because we belong here. The white man says there is freedom and justice for all. We have had "freedom and justice," and that is why we have been almost exterminated. We shall not forget this.
~Grand Council of American Indians, 1927

I had to meet with the same anthropologist a second time, much to my chagrin, and perhaps to hers as well. Thankfully, we have never had to meet since. Ironically years later I became an anthropologist myself because I think it's time for us to save our own stories, our own songs, our own cultural lifeways.

ANTHROPOLOGIST, PART TWO

So, she tells me
During a long discussion
That the government of these United States
Must have had a good reason
For breaking every treaty
They ever signed
With the Native people of this land
I sit there in stunned disbelief
That someone with her education
Someone in a position
That requires her to teach others
Would have such a view
That it could possibly be ok
To break your word time after time
For greed, for gold, for God, for glory
That it would be acceptable
To murder elders, women, and children
For a government based on religious freedom
To deny the first citizens of America
Our religions
All for more land
More gold
More greed
The survivors
Of America's first invasion
Can testify to that
Lies?
We are accustomed to them
We expect them
We're just astounded
That they never end.
Time does not heal all wounds.

HEAL IT OR GIVE IT BACK

You stole this land
You stole this land
You stole this land
Now you demand that we comply
To every law that you can think of
To keep the salmon for yourself
While pouring insecticides and plutonium
Into the once mighty Columbia River
You stole this land
Because you said that we
Weren't utilizing the land
"Properly"
Not like you
By covering it with concrete
Stifling the air with pollution
From your factories
From your SUVs
From your nuclear power plants

You stole this land
A pristine wilderness
Filled with wolves, bears, coyotes
Antelope, salmon, lamprey
Buffalo, eagles, bighorn sheep
Mountain goats once roamed the Gorge
You now claim aren't indigenous
They shouldn't be put back into the Columbia Gorge
Because they might eat endangered plants
Tell me
Please
Who among your group
Is indigenous to this part of the world?
Who caused those plants
To become endangered?
Who hunted the goats until there were no more?
Who caused the extinction
And endangerment of too many species?
All across this continent
Not us

You stole this land
To destroy it?
Where is your responsibility?
Why do you have to destroy the earth
To live upon it?
Why can't you live with it?
Why can't you live within the circle of life
The web that connects us all?

When will you learn that you cannot eat money
Can't breathe it
It doesn't love you
It doesn't miss you when you're gone
But if you continue to pollute everything around you
You will succeed

In polluting everyone
As well as yourself
You stole this land
Invaded, starving on the barren rocks of the Eastern coast
We fed you, showed you how to survive
Only to have you subjugate
At virtually every turn
Sought to exterminate as many Native people as you could
Giving you free rein to immigrate at will
Leaving one continent
To the detriment of others
We had a poor immigration policy back then
And couldn't care less now
As you rant about our neighbors to the south
At least they are from our continent
Our southern brothers and sisters
Also indigenous
Also hunted down like animals

You stole this land
You stole this land
You stole this land
Heal it or give it back!

Dedicated to Clarissa Bertha

The myth is that people came to America for religious freedom. The reality is that the Pilgrims had religious freedom in Holland and disliked the fact their children were adopting cultural norms from Holland. They came to America to isolate their children and keep them from the cultural ways of others.

In a country supposedly founded on the principal of religious freedom, Native people suffered from religious persecution and suppression and received freedom of religion with the passage of the American Indian Religious Freedom Act of 1978, further strengthened by the AIRFA Amendment, public law 103-344, signed by President William Jefferson Clinton in 1994.

THE PILGRIMS

They wanted the land
From sea to shining sea
And they left only pockets
For you and me

Treaties and promises
Supreme Court decisions
Fall swiftly when gold or profit calls
Encouraging expansion and revisions
More and more invaded our shores

Manifest Destiny! was the cry
It led to our imprisonment
It led to our imprisonment
Blanketed us with disease and starvation

Brought to the verge of extinction
The loss of millions of lives, virtual genocide
Brought to this by greed
Or man's inhumanity to man

INNOCENCE

Colored said the Pastor, so long ago
What color? the little boy asked
Loudly, during church services.
Catching one word in the sermon.
Were they pink? the boy asked, curiously,
Were they green?
His confusion a mirror of my own
My embarrassment highlighting me
Laughter filled the church
Awareness crept in, and light
He is right, said the Pastor,
What does it matter, what color?

WHITE GIRL

Hanging in the chat room, telling me how it is
Saying get over it, past is past
I say past is present, we are a part
Of those who have gone before
We carry them within us
Their dreams, their hopes, their fears
Should we forget where we come from
What they gave for us?
Forget that they fought to protect this land
Fought to protect each other from invaders?
Should we forget that the U.S. government
Wanted us exterminated, to the last woman and child?
These United States… Yes, we love our country
We love our land
We do not forget.

If we can learn to accept and enjoy our differences and our commonalities, what kind of world can we create from such friendship, from such unity?

TEACHER

Teach the truth to the children
We are not yet gone
Teach them to protect what is theirs
Tell them that we fought to save our own
Just as their parents would do
If America were invaded today
We were not, are not, brutal savages
That they see portrayed on TV
No stereotypes live here
Just people like you and me
Teach them about Sand Creek
Little Big Horn
The Trail of Tears
Wounded Knee
All we ask for is the truth
After so many lies
Is that too much to ask?

We must protect the forests for our children, grandchildren and children yet to be born. We must protect the forests for those who can't speak for themselves such as the birds, animals, fish and trees.
~Qwatsinas (Hereditary Chief Edward Moody),
  Nuxalk Nation

THE BIRTHDAY

A new day dawned brightly
      the promise of life renewed sparkled from the dew on every leaf
A cry pierced the early morning air
      the sound of a newborn babe
The mother cradled her child gently in her arms
      looking down on the newest member of her tribe
Seeing the dark, solemn eyes widen at her gaze
      she spoke softly to calm and reassure
The thick thatch of black hair stood boldly aloft
      she smoothed it with a soft caress from her work-hardened hands
Her husband strode into the tipi
      to gaze with pride at his child
He reached for the babe with hands that were swift
      and sure when facing an enemy
Suddenly those hands trembled when he touched the infant
      gently, tenderly, he held the babe, smiling down with evident pride
Looking at his weary wife, his eyes spoke for him
      conveying his pride and love
Enveloping her in a blanket of furs
      he laid the babe in her arms
Then he knelt down and pulled them both against his chest
      protectively, lovingly, cradling them
As the sun rose, word spread through the village
      of the birth, a child who would someday lead his people
Now lies safely in his mother's arms.

The Sioux Indians of Minnesota must be exterminated or driven forever beyond the borders of the state.
~Governor Alexander Ramsey, September 9, 1862

HEROES RISE, HEROES FALL

I see history books differently than most
  Your textbooks glorify the roles of your ancestors
Making us appear as savages, brutal, untrustworthy
  Turning your invading ancestors into mighty heroes
Abraham Lincoln painted as the Great Emancipator
  Freeing the slaves while the world watched
Killing the Indians as he pursued genocide from sea
  To shining sea
The great L. Frank Baum, writer of the Wizard of Oz
  Promoter of Indian extermination
Abraham Lincoln was my hero for so long
  As a child…
Until I grew and learned of the 38 Native men
  He sentenced to hang for defending their land
The largest mass hanging
  In the history of the United States of America
As a child Oz was my escape
  Until I found Baum's published editorials
He promoted *total annihilation of the few remaining Indians*
  As a way to secure land from those who lived upon it first
Mark Twain… ah, the profound sadness it brought to my heart
  To read of his belief in Indian extermination
Andrew Jackson, the great Indian fighter
  Denying the Cherokee their Supreme Court decision
Driving them to death on the Trail of Tears
  Heroism is relative, don't believe all the hype
We all have heroes, we all have misconceptions
  We have a responsibility to learn the truth
We have the right to demand the truth.

I was warmed by the sun, rocked by the winds and sheltered by the trees as other Indian babes. I can go everywhere with a good feeling.
~Geronimo [Goyathlay], Chiracahua Apache

SECURITY

The dust beneath my moccasins
        the rock against my back
                protecting me
against the elements
        the wind
              the sand
                      the sun
such a simple thing
        such a gift
              the rock.

When it comes time to die, be not like those whose hearts are filled with the fear of death, so when their time comes they weep and pray for a little more time to live their lives over again in a different way. Sing your death song, and die like a hero going home.
~Chief Aupumut, Mohican

ETERNAL SONG

I feel the song
      of a thousand years
I smell the earth
      of my ancestors
I see the sky
      that looked on other nations
I hear the song
      that carries us through the ages
I taste the victory
      so long denied.

On November 29, 1864, a heinous massacre occurred in Colorado. There was a congressional investigation into this event and it was recognized for what it truly was, a shameful moment in the history of the invasion and occupation of the Americas. The outcome of this massacre was an admission by the federal government that it should not have happened and a treaty was signed, granting reparations for the destruction of our village and the murders of our people, many of whom were shot in the back while fleeing with their hands held high to indicate surrender.

We are still fighting in the courts to have that promise, that treaty, the contractual agreement with the United States federal government, fulfilled today.

The dedication for the Sand Creek Memorial National Site was on April 28, 2007.

The dedication, which consisted of about 1,000 people, included Sand Creek descendants, several senators, representatives and Tribal leaders who spoke at the event.

I acknowledge and admit wrongs were done by the federal government or tolerated by the federal government here and across the nation, said Presidential candidate Senator Sam Brownback of Kansas, who also attended the memorial dedication ceremony.

Bill Dawson, a former ranch owner whose grandfather homesteaded the land in 1903 said, *You know, there are still people who say it was a battle and not a massacre. They probably don't believe in the Holocaust either.* Dawson was diligent about protecting what he knew was an important historical site, so protective that he ended up in jail after a face-off with trespassers. Unfortunately, not all the ranchers in the area have been willing to part with land that victims' descendants consider part of the original site.

Horwitz, Tony. "The Horrific Sand Creek Massacre Will Be Forgotten No More." *Smithsonian.com*. Smithsonian Institution, 01 Dec. 2014. Web. 14 May 2017.

This poem was written at the behest of my grandfather, Eugene Blackbear, Sr., and is dedicated to him. Thank you, Numshim, for your stories, your teachings, and your love.

SAND CREEK MASSACRE

All that is necessary for the triumph of evil is for good men to do nothing.
~Edmund Burke

With the mist rising
From the frozen winter Colorado ground
On a bend in the Sand Creek
600 people peacefully camped
At the request and invitation
Of the U.S. Army
Telling us to camp near Fort Lyon
To be *under the protection of Fort Lyon*

Led by those in agreement of peace
We followed their request
Moving our people within 40 miles of the fort
Sending our men east to hunt buffalo
While 600 people, women, children and elders
With some 35 men
Stayed behind in camp

Trusting our safety to the White Man's word
So trusting that we posted no guard
The only warning we had on that long ago winter sunrise
Hooves falling on the frozen land
Some thought it was buffalo
Then women cried out,
Soldiers!

Awakened abruptly,
Confusion broke out
Many people, barely dressed
ran to imagined safety

Hundreds rallied to Chief Black Kettle's camp
He held a lodge pole high in his hands
Flying bravely from that pole
The large garrison flag gifted to the Cheyenne
At a meeting between Abraham Lincoln and
Our Chiefs, Black Kettle, Roman Nose and others
Colonel Greenwood
Assured us
We would be safe

Protected as long as we stood
Under the American flag

Women, children, elders
Ran to stand beneath promised safety
Invoked by that American flag

Beneath that flag
Was another
The white flag of truce

Do not be afraid cried Black Kettle to our people
The soldiers will not hurt you!
Then they opened fire...
On unarmed women, children of all ages
On peaceful chiefs and slow-moving elders

Bullets flying
Soldiers dismounting to fire howitzers
Upon the once sleeping village
Towards the hundreds of women and children now gathered
Beneath that American flag

A 75-year old man
Singing as he faced over 700 troops
Saying, *Stop, STOP!*
With his hands held high
Then White Antelope sang...
Nothing lives long
Only the earth and the mountains
The death song of the Cheyenne

They fired on him
Shot down an unarmed grandfather
He sang...
Nothing lives long
Only the earth and the mountains

White Antelope's testicles
Cut off by a soldier

Who bragged to his comrades of
His plans to make a tobacco pouch
From his gruesome trophy

Colonel Chivington
Methodist Minister
Man of god
Man of the cloth
Man of blood and death
On that bitter cold winter morning
Commanded those troops
Against those who knew we were peaceful
Those who recognized the flag of truce
Those few among the troops who sought
To end the madness

Bullets flew among those huddled beneath that flag
The people ran to freedom
To imagined safety

35 men left at camp ran seeking weapons,
Any weapon
To fight this unexpected attack
Protect elders, children, women
Who ran screaming in fear
The men cried out to the women to come to them
As they formed a circle around them
To protect them with their own bodies

People who ran with their arms raised in surrender
Were shot in the back trying to escape
Many hiding under the banks of the creek
Eventually women came out
Lifting their dresses to reveal themselves as women
When soldiers approached
Were shot down as they stood there
Skin bare in winter's stark light
Shot down and desecrated as soldiers took "trophies"
From the defenseless bodies of the many women
Of all ages

Proof they killed women
Cut from the bodies of their victims
Soldiers draped women's breasts and montes
Over the pommels of their saddles

Those who later sought to "civilize" us
Cut off the penises and testicles of the men as well
None were safe that morning
Not elders, not women, not children
Certainly not warriors
Not one Native person was left un-scalped

With razor sharp sabers
Infants cut from the safety of their mother's bodies
Swung by their tiny feet
Heads dashed against the rocks
Left to die in the bitterness
Of that late November winter sun

Our men dug pits in the dry creek bed
To defend the flight of those running to safety
Our weapons puny against the might
Of the troops
Of Colonel Chivington

Our few men who remained fought for hours,
When the "battle" was over
those who survived escaped
As had the women, children and elders
Who had run away in terror

People ran toward the east
To where our hunters had gone
Blood frozen on our bodies
Clothing left far behind
In what was left of our homes
Now ransacked, looted, and destroyed
We ran to safety, barefoot, wounded and stunned
No food, nothing to bandage our wounds

50 miles to the safety of our men
50 miles in the icy cold Colorado winter
Bitter winds whipping us on our way

We straggled into the hunting camp
Our men shocked at our sudden appearance
Shock followed by tears of heartbreak
Tears of warriors, men hardened by battle
By time, by culture, their own egos
Tears of the warriors fell like rain

Over 100 women and children
And 28 men
Lay in that camp
Far behind us now
Where we had promised to go
Where the white man had promised us
Safety and peace
On that long ago winter morning
November 29, 1864
Our Pearl Harbor,
Our 9/11
One of many...

BIO

Renée Roman Nose, M.A.I.S., enrolled member of the Cheyenne and Arapaho Tribes of Oklahoma, is an activist, actor, artist, and cultural anthropologist. She played Camille in "Some Days are Better Than Others" (2010), has done commercial, voice, radio, modeling, and live performances, including stand up comedy. She is President of Fierce Courage, providing team building, wellness facilitation and motivational speaking. An international speaker with a solid reputation for informative and interesting lectures, Ms. Roman Nose has more than 25 years of experience in front of appreciative audiences.

ACKNOWLEDGMENTS

Thanks to the editors of the following journals and books in which these poems first appeared in whole or in part. Parts of *Sweet Grass Talking* were originally self-published.

"Have Warpaint-Will Travel," *NAME*, Portland, OR. (2014). Print.

"Round Dance," *Eleven Magazine*, Orlando, FL. (1995). Print.

"Sweet Grass Talking," *NAME*, Portland, OR (2007). Print.

"A Twisted Tale," *Quality of Life: Achieving Balance in an Unbalanced World*, by Dr. H. Stanley Jones, Kauai Museum Shop, Kauai, HI. (1994). Print.

"Vows," *Prism Magazine*, Oregon State University, Corvallis, OR. (2008). Print.

Made in the USA
Middletown, DE
25 October 2020